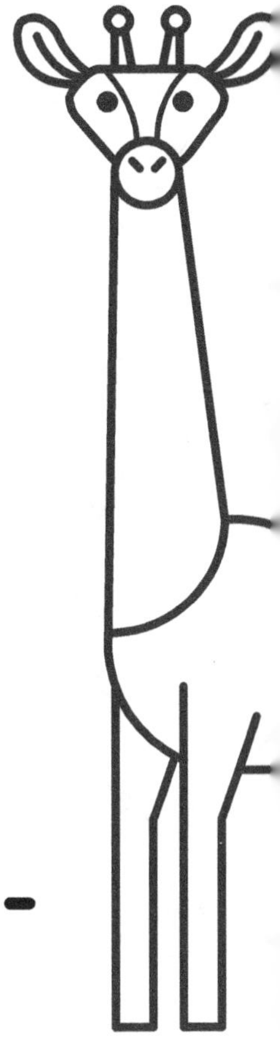

THIS BOOK BELONGS TO

____

PRACTICE CUTTING LINES

PRACTICE CUTTING SHAPES

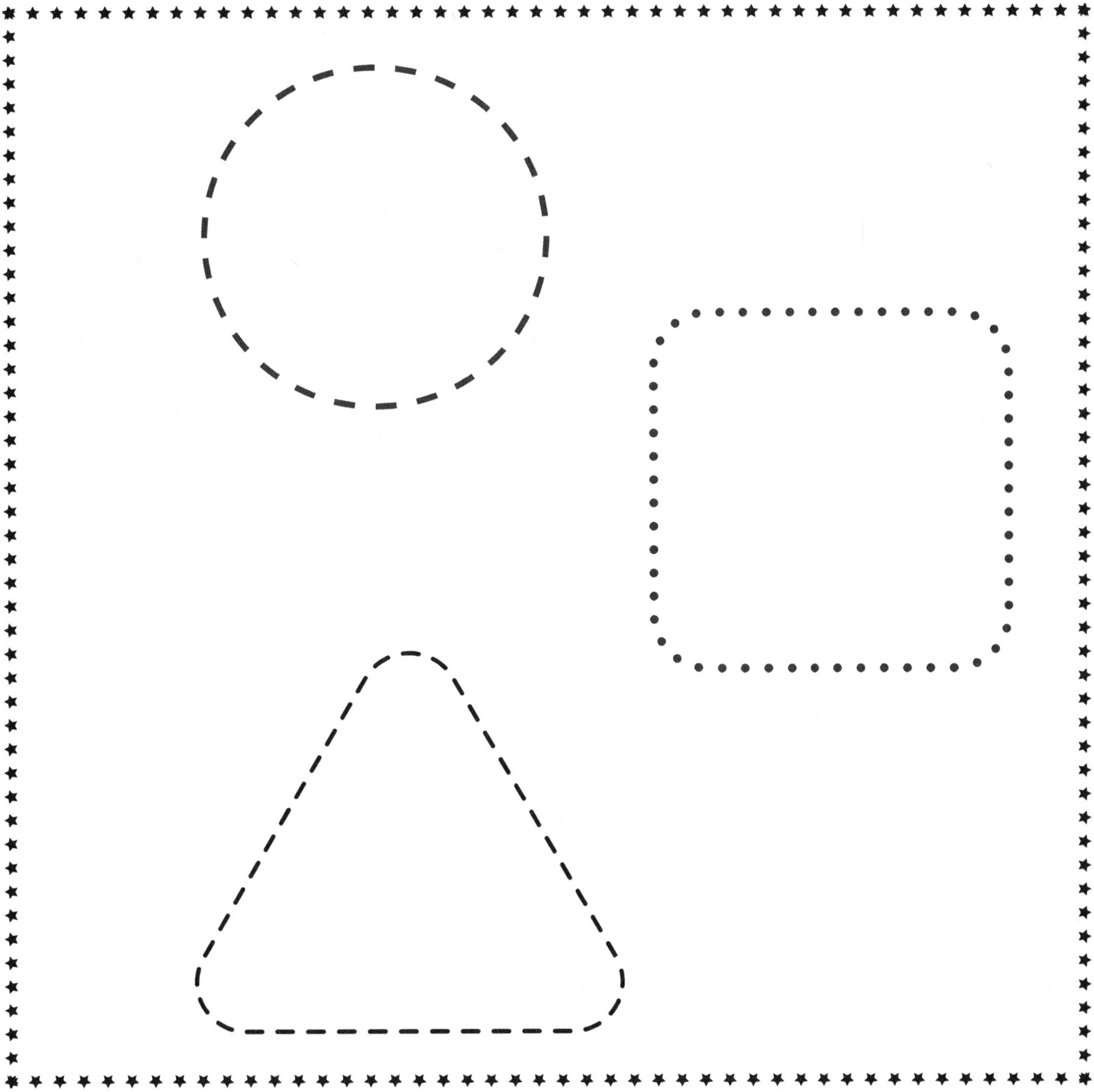

PRACTICE CUTTING STARS

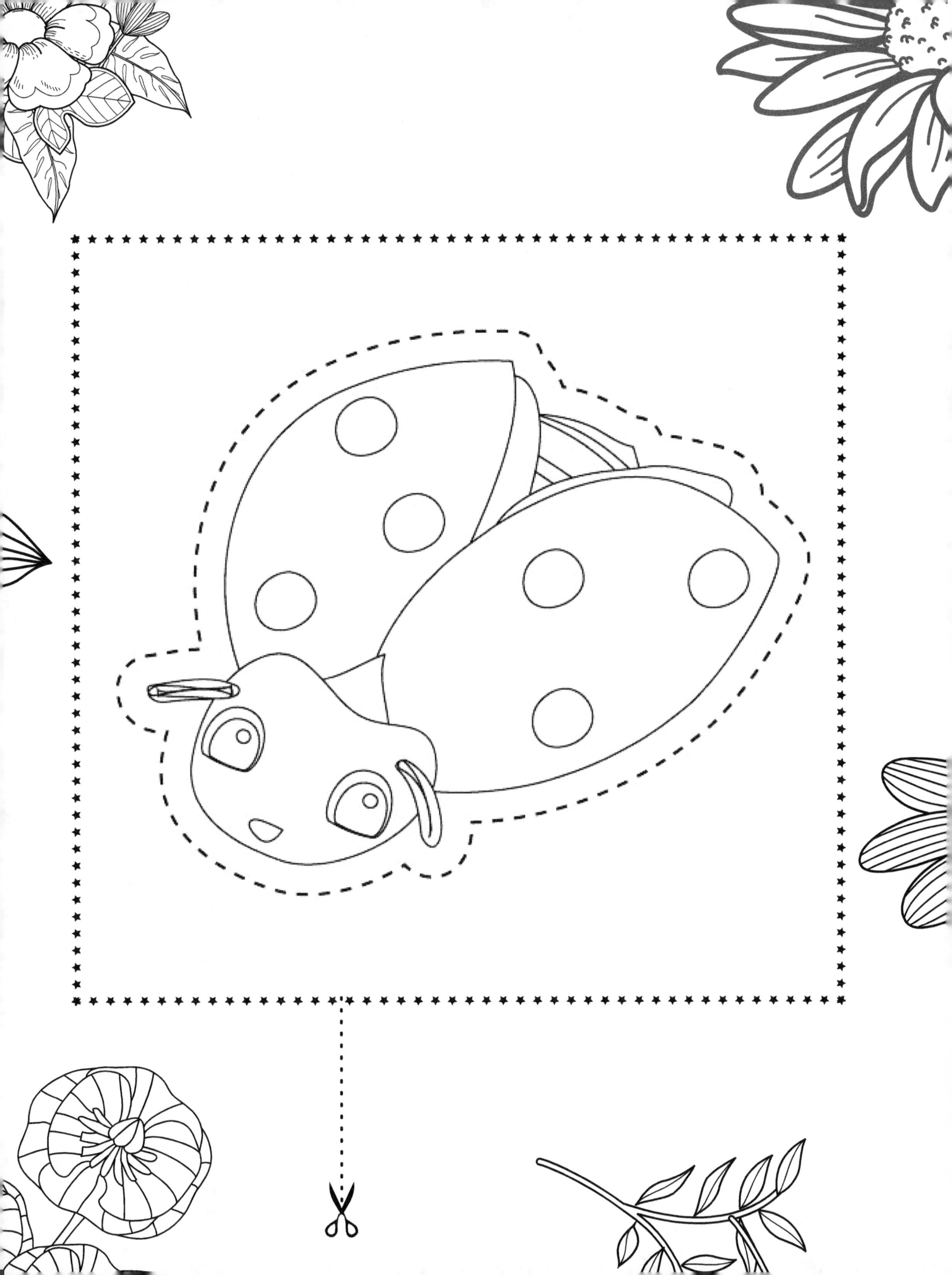

www.ingramcontent.com/pod-product-compliance
Lightning Source LLC
Chambersburg PA
CBHW060000230526
45472CB00008B/1878
9798415805396